Copyright © 2021 by Gahmya Drummond-Bey

All rights reserved.

Library of Congress Control Number:
ISBN: 978-1-7335569-8-9

Published by Evolved Teacher Press.

No part of this publication may be reproduced, stored, or transmitted in any form or by any means, electronic, mechanical, photocopying, recording, scanning, or otherwise, except as permitted under Section 107 or 108 of the 1976 United States Copyright Act, without the prior written permission of the author. Requests to the author and publisher for permission should be addressed to the following email: gahmya@evolvedteacher.com

Limitation of liability/disclaimer of warranty: While the publisher and author have used their best efforts in preparing this guide and workbook, they make no representations or warranties with respect to the accuracy or completeness of the contents of this document and specifically disclaim any implied warranties of merchantability or fitness for particular purpose. No warranty may be created or extended by sales representatives, promoters, or written sales materials.

Due to the dynamic nature of the Internet, certain links and website information contained in this publication may have changed. The author and publisher make no representations to the current accuracy of the web information shared.

I hope every time you pick up this book, your hands are filled with magic and your heart is filled with love.

Today is an exciting day! It's a day when the young person in your life has another chance to connect learning with fun. I call that "Flearning."

Flearning is when Fun and Learning come together to create a thirst for even more knowledge.

Young people are sponges and learning new things is a natural curiosity. However, it's also important to add enthusiasm, play, and topics of interest.

Children all over the world, as young as four years old, have learned to write with this book and format. Now, educators and families across the globe use this (and our digital courses) to teach young children. Although this book is recommended for ages 7-9, older students also use this book to build a foundation for writing and form a passion of expression they may not have had before.

To the adult who sees this and thinks, "My kid could never do that," just try it! Kids are spectacular!

www.kidYOUniversity.com

Go to our website for access to the digital course that accompanies this book!

Meet Nyota!

Hi Friend! My name is Nyota!

I love animals! Let's write all about some of the most interesting animals in the world!

In this book, you will learn about some really cool animals! You will also learn to write a paragraph from what you've learned! When you learn how to write your ideas clearly, you can write books with them. Then, people can read your ideas all over the world!

Meet Miss Hamburger!

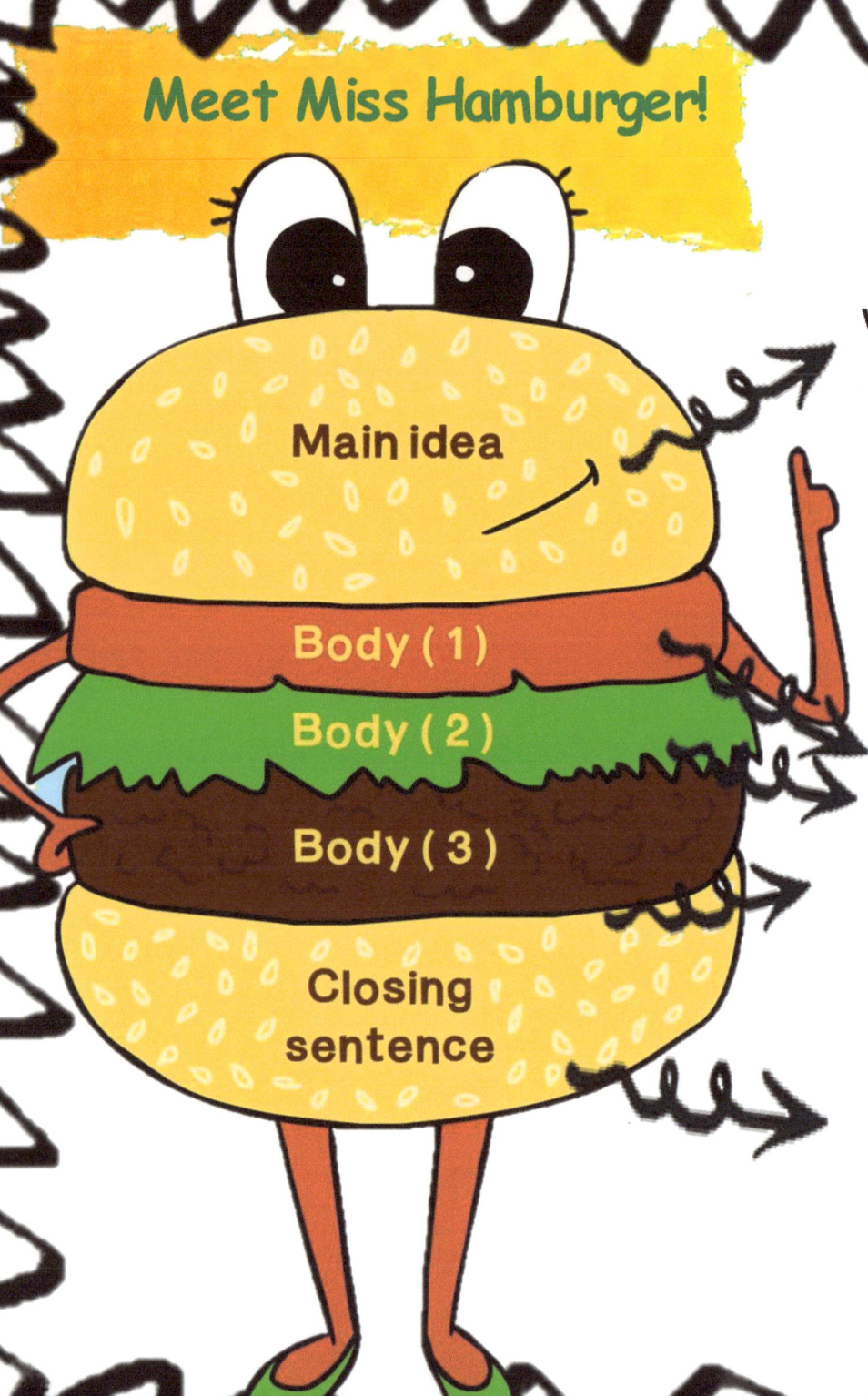

My name is Miss Hamburger! Today, I wore my special hamburger dress. My Hamburger dress helps you to remember what a paragraph is. A paragraph is a group of sentences that tell about one idea.

A very clear paragraph has 8 sentences.

The first sentence is your topic sentence. The topic sentence tells the main idea. That's what you're writing about!

After that, you have 3 more sentences that are called body sentences. The body sentences tell "Why" and "How." Each body sentence also has a best friend, called an example sentence. There are 3 example sentences.

Last, we have our closing sentence. The closing sentence just tells the reader what you are thinking one more time!

PRACTICE

Let's learn about Quokkas!

Quokkas live in Australia.

They are called "the happiest animals on Earth." People call them happy because it looks like they are always smiling.

A baby quokka is called a "joey." Quokkas are herbivores. An herbivore is an animal that only eats plants and does not eat meat.
Quokkas eat grass, stems, and bark.

They are also nocturnal. Nocturnal animals stay awake at night and sleep during the day. Quokkas do not have very long lives. They live for about 10 years.
Many people say that quokkas look like small kangaroos. They are also marsupials, just like kangaroos! A marsupial is an animal that has a pouch for its baby.

Quokkas are very interesting!

Let's write a paragraph about quokkas!

Topic: Why are quokkas interesting?

- Main idea
- Body (1)
- Body (2)
- Body (3)
- Closing sentence

Quokkas are interesting **for many reasons.**

First, quokkas are interesting because they are **happy**.

For example, their mouths look like they are always smiling!

Next, quokkas are interesting because they are **nocturnal**.

For example, they sleep in the day and are awake all night.

Finally, quokkas are interesting because they have **short lives**.

For example, they only live for about ten years.

Quokkas are so cool!

Put the paragraph in order. Write 1, 2, 3, 4, 5, 6, 7, or 8 in the box next to the sentence.

☐ For example, they only live for about ten years.

☐ First, Quokkas are interesting because they are happy.

☐ For example, they stay awake at night and sleep during the day.

☐ Finally, quokkas are interesting because they have short lives.

[1] Quokkas are interesting for many reasons.

☐ For example, their mouths always look like they are smiling.

☐ Next, Quokkas are interesting because they are nocturnal.

☐ Quokkas are so cool!

Your turn!

Why are quokkas interesting?

BRAINSTORMING

Quokkas are _____ for _____ many reasons.

First, _____ are interesting because _____

For example, _____

Quokkas

Next, _____ are interesting because _____

For example, _____

DRAW

Use your paragraph to draw pictures.
(Show each of your reasons.)

FIRST,

NEXT,

FINALLY,

Now that you understand how to write a paragraph, let's practice some more. We will also learn about some more super cool animals!

Table of Contents

 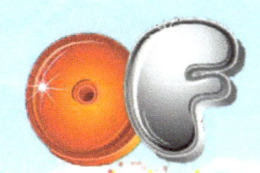 Let's learn about tardigrades.

 Let's learn about tarsiers.

 Let's learn about star-nosed moles.

 Let's learn about alpacas.

 Let's learn about dumbo octopuses.

 Let's learn about blobfish.

 Let's learn about flying foxes.

 Let's learn about emperor penguins.

Let's learn about the tardigrade!

Tardigrades are also called "water bears." Many people think they are cute because they look like little bears that live in the water. Tardigrades are great swimmers. They usually live in lakes, oceans, and ponds.

They eat plants and tiny worms. Animals that eat meat and plants are called "omnivores." Tardigrades have eight legs. The name Tardigrade came from the word "Tardigrada."

"Tardigrada" is an Italian word (from Italy) and it means "slow walker." Tardigrades are very slow!

They are also strong! They can live even if they do not have food for ten years! Tardigrades can also live in boiling water and extremely cold weather! Tardigrades are interesting because they can survive almost anything! It is very difficult for a tardigrade to die.

Lesson 1. Why are tardigrades interesting?

BRAINSTORMING

Tardigrades are _____ for _____ many reasons.

First, _____ are interesting because _____

For example, _____

Keep Going!

Next, _____

are interesting because _____

_____

_____

For example, _____

_____

_____

_____

Use your paragraph to draw pictures.
(Show each of your reasons.)

FIRST,

NEXT,

FINALLY,

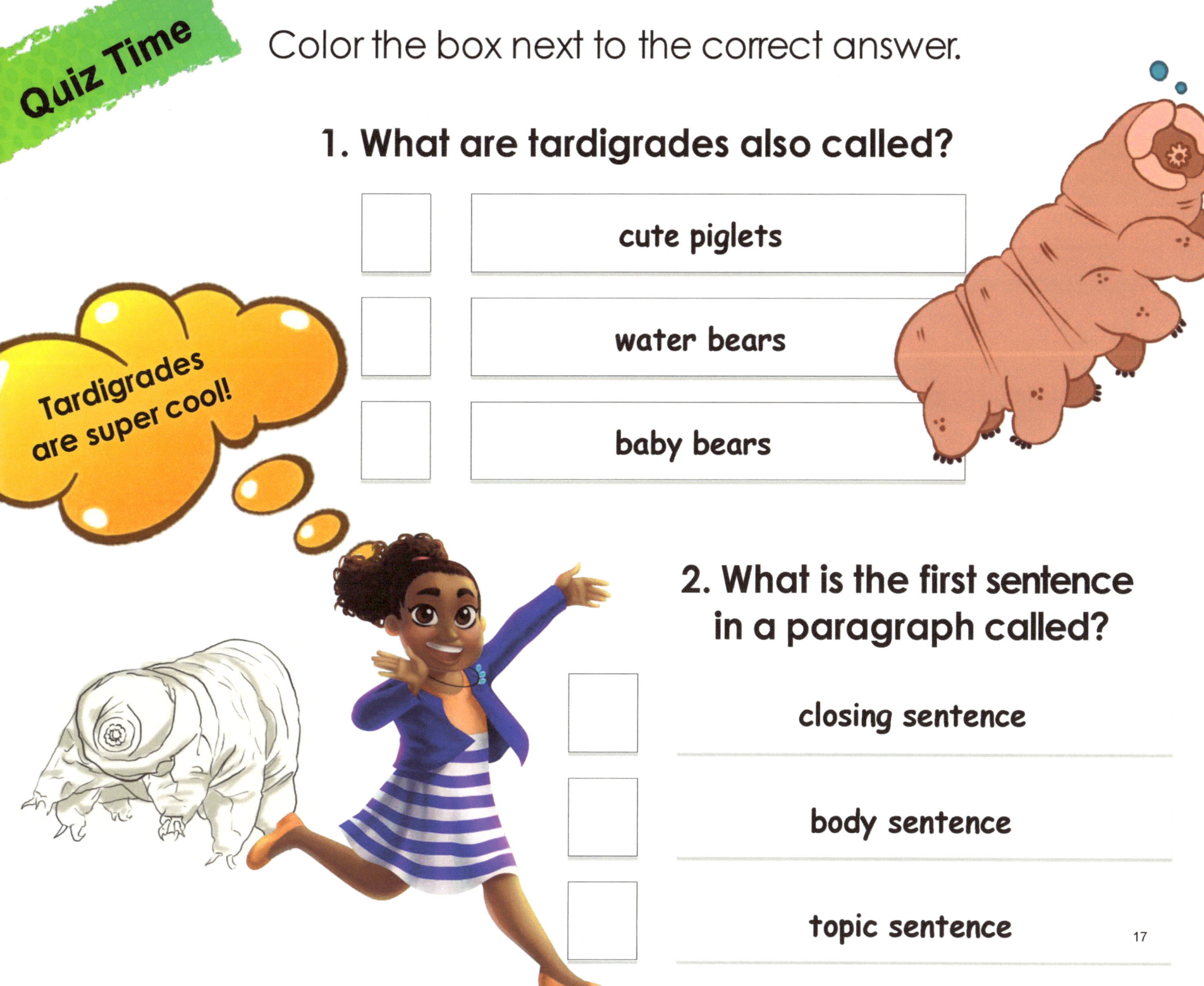

The Tarsier is so cool!

carnivore

small

flexible

nocturnal

Tarsiers live in Asia. You can find them in a country called The Philippines. It is very hot in the Philippines. Tarsiers love hot weather. Tarsiers are small animals with very large eyes. They also have small brains.

In fact, the tarsier's eyes are the same size as its brain!

Its eyeballs do not move. So, if it wants to see something, it has to move its entire head. The tarsier is a carnivore. It eats insects, birds, snakes, lizards, and bats. It is also nocturnal. That means, it stays awake at night an d sleeps during the day.

The tarsier is very sensitive, so if you see one, you have to be very quiet. When some tarsiers are scared, they may bang their heads against a tree and break their skulls!

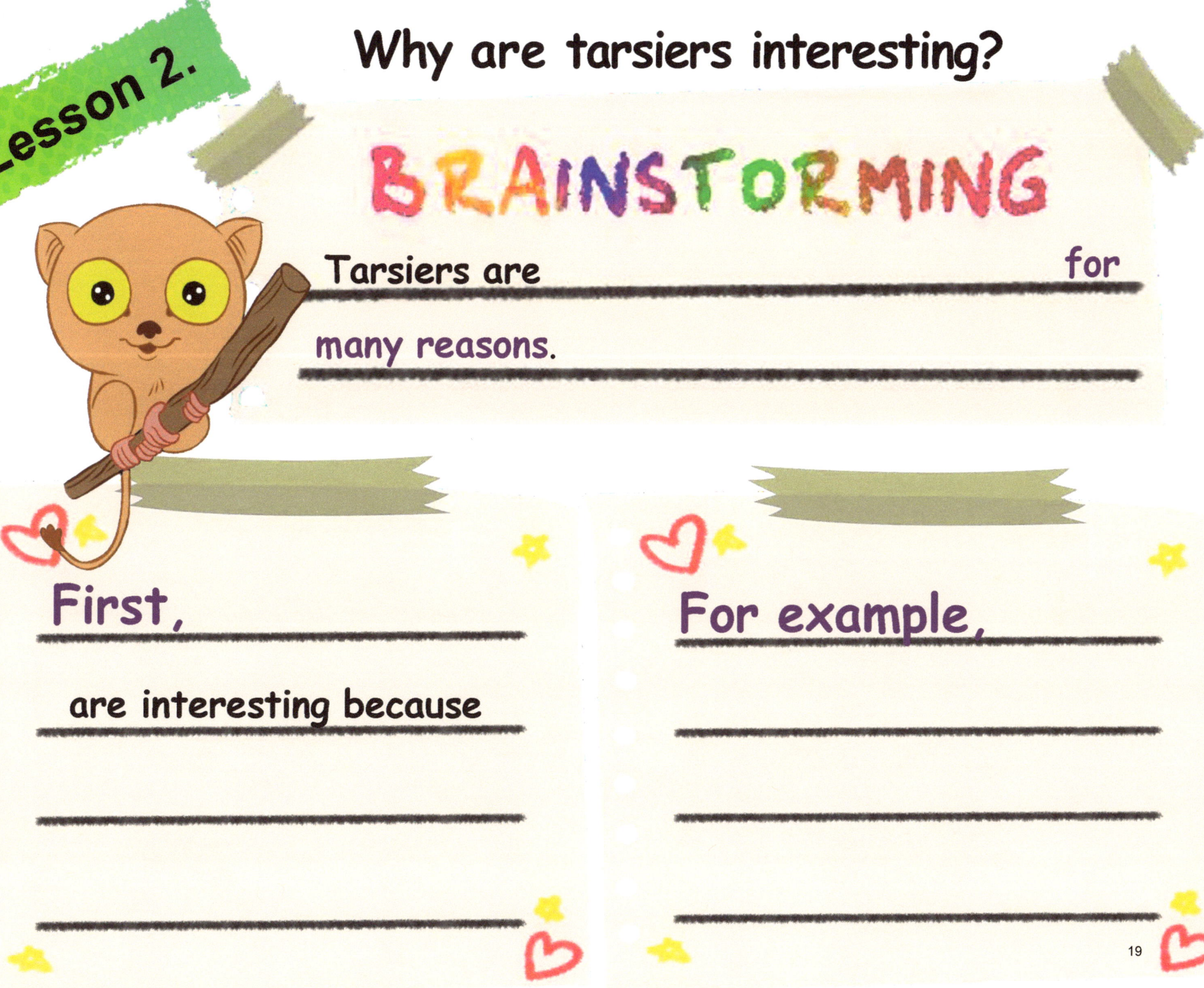

Practice

Next,
_____

are interesting because _____

_____

_____

For example, _____

_____

_____

_____

DRAW

Use your paragraph to draw pictures.
(Show each of your reasons.)

FIRST,

NEXT,

FINALLY,

Quiz Time

Color the box next to the correct answer.

1. What kind of weather do tarsiers like most?

   ☐ Tarsiers prefer hot weather.

   ☐ Tarsiers prefer cold weather.

   ☐ Tarsiers prefer warm weather.

Let's see what you remember!

2. What is the last sentence in a paragraph called?

   ☐ closing sentence

   ☐ body sentence

   ☐ topic sentence

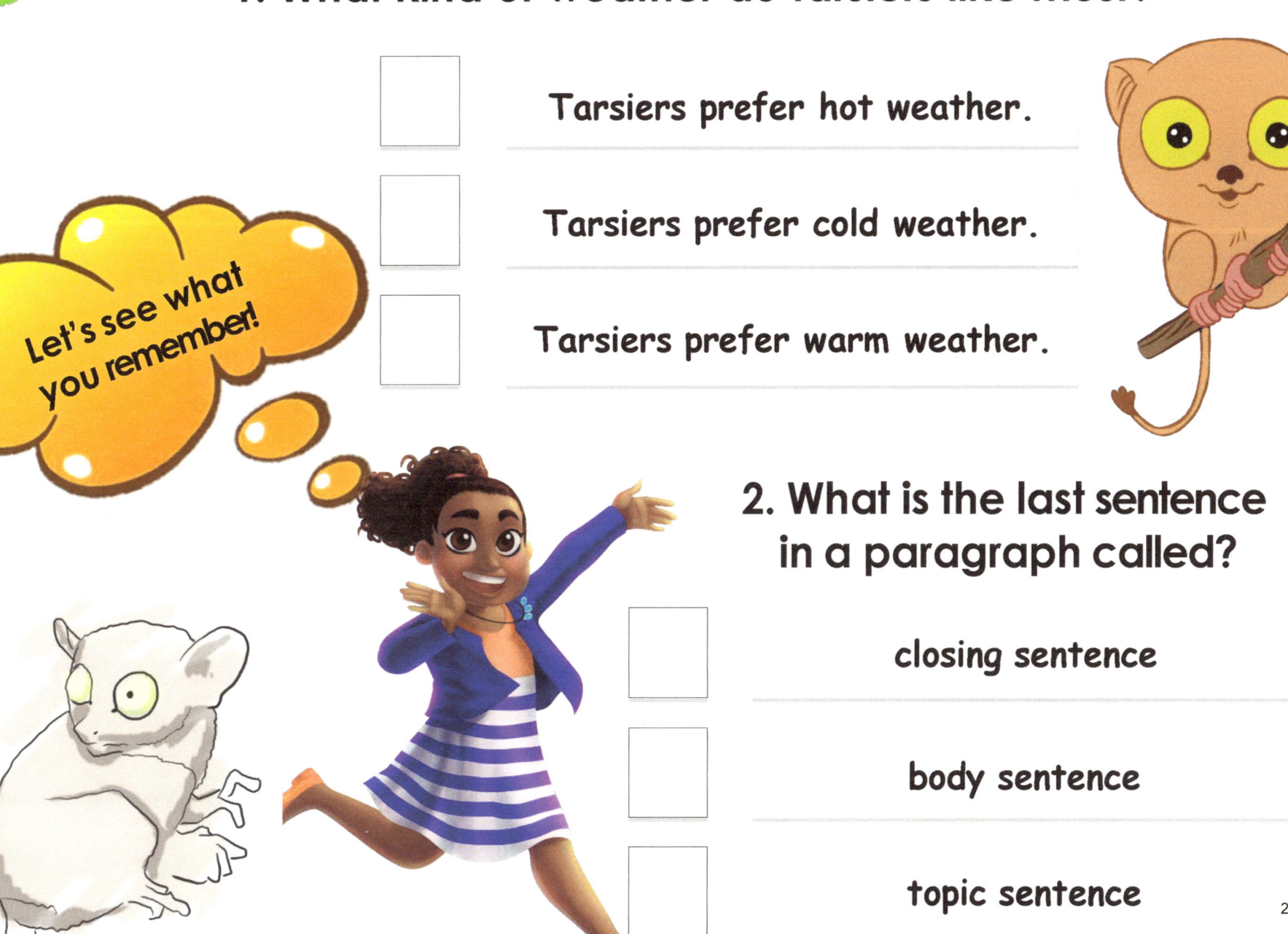

Star-nosed moles are special!

carnivore

small

swims well

almost blind

The **star-nosed mole** lives in The United States and Canada. It is very small. It's almost the size of a hamster.

The star-nosed mole is almost blind. That means it cannot see well and it has very weak eyes. It likes to live in dark places underground. Its nose is called a snout.

It uses its snout to know what and where things are. The star-nosed mole has twenty-two tentacles that stick out of its snout.
So, it uses its snout to smell things and its tentacles to feel things.
It also uses its tentacles to identify food.

The star-nosed mole eats insects, worms, and small fish. It is a carnivore.

It is also a good swimmer.
It lives near places with shallow water, like ponds or streams.

Lesson 3. Why are star-nosed moles interesting?

BRAINSTORMING

Star-nosed moles are _____ for many reasons.

First, _____ are interesting because _____

For example, _____

Keep going!

DRAW

Use your paragraph to draw pictures.
(Show each of your reasons.)

FIRST,

NEXT,

FINALLY,

Quiz Time

Color the box next to the correct answer.

1. How do star-nosed moles know where they are going?

   ☐ They use their eyes to see.

   ☐ They use their snout and tentacles.

   ☐ They wear cute little glasses.

2. How did the star-nosed mole get its name?

   ☐ Its snout looks like a star.

   ☐ It has five noses!

   ☐ Its nose glows like a star.

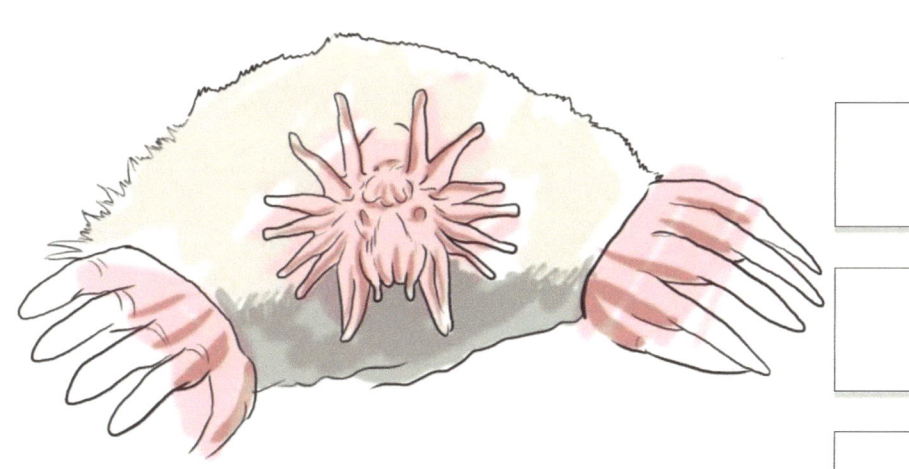

Alpacas are cool for many reasons!

kind

beautiful
careful

herbivore

Alpacas look like small camels without humps. Most alpacas are from South America. A baby alpaca is called a "cria." They are very kind and gentle. But, most alpacas do not like to be grabbed.

Alpacas can live for up to 20 years.
Alpacas are herbivores. They graze and eat grass or hay. Alpacas have to be careful because many plants (like buckwheat and acorns) are poisonous to the alpaca.
Alpacas have very beautiful fiber that is soft like a sheep's wool. Some people shave alpacas' fiber to make blankets, sweaters, socks, and coats.

Lesson 4. Why are alpacas special?

BRAINSTORMING

Practice

DRAW

Use your paragraph to draw pictures.
(Show each of your reasons.)

FIRST,

NEXT,

FINALLY,

Quiz Time

Color the box next to the correct answer.

1. What do alpacas eat?

☐ Alpacas are carnivores.

☐ Alpacas are omnivores.

☐ Alpacas are herbivores.

2. Why do alpacas have to be careful when they eat?

☐ Many plants are poisonous to the alpaca.

☐ Alpacas hunt in scary places.

☐ Alpacas do not have any teeth.

Dumbo Octopuses are special for many reasons!

The **Dumbo Octopus** is a kind of Octopus. Its name comes from Walt Disney's character, Dumbo, which was an elephant with large ears.

This animal can be found in oceans all over the world! They live at the bottom of the sea, so it can be hard to see them.

That's also why they are rare. When an animal is rare, that means it's hard to see one.

Dumbo Octopuses like to live in cold water where there is little light. They cannot survive out of deep water. So, you cannot have one for a pet.

Dumbo Octopuses can be red, green, or orange. They have eight arms and a soft head-shaped body.
The fins at the top of their head look like ears.

The Dumbo Octopus has a short life.

It lives between 3 and 5 years.
It is a carnivore. It eats plankton, crustaceans (crab, lobster, shrimp), and sea worms.

small

rare

carnivore

short life

Lesson 5. For Example

What do you think about Dumbo Octopuses?

Topic sentence

Detail 1 First, dumbo octopuses are _____ because

Example For example,

Detail 2 Next, _____

Example For example, _____

Detail 3 Finally, _____

Example For example, _____

DRAW

Use your paragraph to draw pictures.
(Show each of your reasons.)

FIRST,

NEXT,

FINALLY,

Quiz Time

Color the box next to the correct answer.

1. Why can't you have a dumbo octopus for a pet?

   ☐ They are too cute to be pets.

   ☐ They need to live deep in the ocean.

   ☐ They are very big.

2. What do dumbo octopuses have on top of their heads?

   ☐ Their ears are on top of their heads.

   ☐ Their noses are on top of their heads.

   ☐ Their fins are on top of their heads.

Mirror Time! You have learned so much!

I am so proud of you!
Are you proud of yourself?
1.) Find a mirror.
2.) Stand in front of the mirror.
3.) Say 3 things you are proud of yourself for.
("I am proud of myself for focusing." "I am proud of myself for learning to write paragraphs."
"I am proud of myself for _____.")

Blobfish are interesting for many reasons!

carnivore

rare

(Out of the water)

endangered

(In the water)

The **Blobfish** lives in the deep waters of Australia, Tasmania, and New Zealand. Blobfish are carnivores. That means they eat meat! Blobfish eat deep water crustaceans. A crustacean is a kind of shellfish (a fish that has a shell).

Blobfish are an endangered species because of ocean trawling.

Ocean trawling is when someone has a job to catch fish and puts a large net at the bottom of the ocean to catch the fish that are deep in the sea.

Some people call the blobfish "The World's Ugliest Animal." The blobfish doesn't really have any muscle, so its shape is different in water and out of water.

The blobfish lives deep in the ocean, so it's hard to ever see one

Lesson 6.

What do you think about Blobfish?

Topic sentence

Detail 1   First, Blobfish are _____ because

Example   For example,

Detail 2

_____
_____

Example

_____
_____

Detail 3

_____
_____

Example

_____
_____

DRAW

Use your paragraph to draw pictures.
(Show each of your reasons.)

FIRST,

NEXT,

FINALLY,

Quiz Time

Color the box next to the correct answer.

1. Why are blobfish so squishy out of the water?

☐ They do not have much muscle.

☐ They are made of jelly.

☐ They are crustaceans.

2. Why are blobfish so rare?

☐ They only come out in the summer.

☐ They live deep in the bottom of the ocean.

☐ Blobfish are not rare.

Game Time!

Without reading about blobfish again, could you say **4** facts about blobfish in **one minute**?

Try it!
Set a timer!

Go! Go! Go!

The pteropus (Flying fox) is fascinating for many reasons!

The **pteropus** is the largest bat in the world!

Many people call the pteropus a "flying fox" because it looks like a fox with wings.
Although it is also called a "flying fox," it is not a fox. It is a kind of bat.
Pteropuses are also called "fruit bats."

They live in Southeast Asia, Australia, and East Africa. The "flying fox" enjoys tropical places.

It is an herbivore. It eats nectar, blossom, pollen, and fruit. Sometimes, flying foxes eat insects. But, they usually do not because they prefer not to eat meat.

The flying fox is an endangered species. Many people in the Mariana Islands enjoy eating flying fox meat.

Also, some people hunt the flying fox because it eats the crops that farmers are trying to grow.

Pteropuses (flying foxes) are not birds.
They are flying mammals. Pteropuses are nocturnal. They usually find food at night.

They have strong eyesight and a strong sense of smell.

nocturnal

large

herbivore

 **DRAW**

Use your paragraph to draw pictures.
(Show each of your reasons.)

FIRST,

NEXT,

FINALLY,

Quiz Time

Color the box next to the correct answer.

1. What are some of pteropuses other names?

☐ They are called flying mice and big babies.

☐ They are called flying foxes and fruit bats.

☐ They are called flying monkeys and big birds.

2. What kind of animals are pteropuses?

☐ They are birds.

☐ They are foxes.

☐ They are mammals.

Emperor Penguins are incredible for many reasons!

huge

cute

carnivore

flightless

responsible

Emperor Penguins are huge!

The Emperor Penguin is the tallest and heaviest of all of the penguins. They can also dive deeper than all of the other birds and all of the other kinds of penguins.

Emperor Penguins are flightless. They cannot fly, but they can swim. They usually live in Antarctica.

Emperor penguins do not like to live alone. They live in groups called a colony. Emperor penguins do not build nests. The mommies lay one egg. Then, the mommies go away and find food.

The emperor penguin daddies take care of the egg until it becomes a baby penguin. That's why some people say that Emperor penguin dads are the best dads in the world!

A baby emperor penguin is called a "chick," just like many other baby birds.

The daddy Emperor Penguins do not eat any food until the mommy Emperor Penguins return with food. Mommy penguins are great hunters and bring fish for the family to eat. Penguins are carnivores. Their poop is pink because of the kind of sea animals they eat.

Lesson 8.

Why are emperor penguins incredible?

DRAW

**Use your paragraph to draw pictures.
(Show each of your reasons.)**

FIRST,

NEXT,

FINALLY,

Quiz Time

Color the box next to the correct answer.

1. What color is emperor penguin poop?

☐ brown

☐ blue

☐ pink

2. What are baby emperor penguins called?

☐ Baby emperor penguins are called chicks.

☐ Baby emperor penguins are called kids.

☐ Baby emperor penguins are called kittens.

How will you celebrate?

Today, I will
_____

because I did a **great job** and I wrote a paragraph by myself!

sign:_____

www.kidYOUniversity.com

www.ingramcontent.com/pod-product-compliance
Lightning Source LLC
Chambersburg PA
CBHW041150070526

44583CB00004B/135